W9-ACR-318

BEATING BULLYING™

HOW TO BEAT SOCIAL ALIENATION

JASON PORTERFIELD

rosen publishing's
rosen central®

NEW YORK

Published in 2013 by The Rosen Publishing Group, Inc.
29 East 21st Street, New York, NY 10010

Copyright 2013 by The Rosen Publishing Group, Inc.

First Edition

Library of Congress Cataloging-in-Publication Data

Porterfield, Jason.
How to beat social alienation/Jason Porterfield.—1st ed.
    p. cm.—(Beating bullying)
Includes bibliographical references and index.
ISBN 978-1-4488-6812-4 (library binding)—
ISBN 978-1-4488-6821-6 (pbk.)—
ISBN 978-1-4488-6822-3 (6-pack)
1. Alienation (Social psychology) 2. Behavior modification. I. Title.
HM1131.P67 2013
302.5'44—dc23

2012003928

Manufactured in the United States of America

CPSIA Compliance Information: Batch #S12YA: For further information, contact Rosen Publishing, New York, New York, at 1-800-237-9932.

CONTENTS

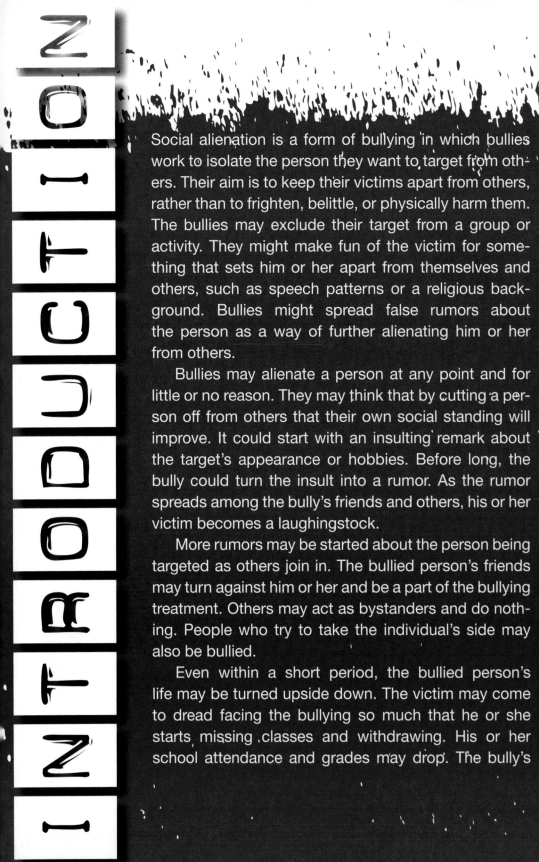

INTRODUCTION

Social alienation is a form of bullying in which bullies work to isolate the person they want to target from others. Their aim is to keep their victims apart from others, rather than to frighten, belittle, or physically harm them. The bullies may exclude their target from a group or activity. They might make fun of the victim for something that sets him or her apart from themselves and others, such as speech patterns or a religious background. Bullies might spread false rumors about the person as a way of further alienating him or her from others.

Bullies may alienate a person at any point and for little or no reason. They may think that by cutting a person off from others that their own social standing will improve. It could start with an insulting remark about the target's appearance or hobbies. Before long, the bully could turn the insult into a rumor. As the rumor spreads among the bully's friends and others, his or her victim becomes a laughingstock.

More rumors may be started about the person being targeted as others join in. The bullied person's friends may turn against him or her and be a part of the bullying treatment. Others may act as bystanders and do nothing. People who try to take the individual's side may also be bullied.

Even within a short period, the bullied person's life may be turned upside down. The victim may come to dread facing the bullying so much that he or she starts missing classes and withdrawing. His or her school attendance and grades may drop. The bully's

Social alienation can make the bullying target feel cut off from his or her classmates. The bullied person may lose self-confidence and withdraw further from others.

target may become so depressed that he or she harms others or attempts suicide.

Social alienation can be challenging to beat, particularly without help. However, it is possible to overcome bullying behavior through hard work and patience. Because awareness of the harmful effects of social alienation has grown, there are more places to go for help in beating the bullies.

CHAPTER 1

A HIDDEN PAIN

Many people face bullying every day. Bullying takes many forms. It can begin as seemingly harmless teasing, or it can turn nasty right away. It is such a common practice that many adults see bullying as an ordinary part of growing up.

WHAT IS BULLYING?

Bullying is unwanted, abusive behavior directed at a person by another individual or by a group of people. Usually, it is seen as a way to make the bully feel powerful while the bully's target feels weak.

Bullying can be physical, verbal, or psychological (when the bully uses ways to control or change a person's relationships with peers). Bullying can range from such behavior as name-calling or physical attacks to more subtle forms. Direct physical and verbal abuse are the most obvious forms of bullying and are also the forms that can most easily be combated by teachers,

Teachers may have a hard time seeing social alienation as it is taking place. This kind of bullying can be difficult to correct if the target does not tell someone what is happening.

parents, or friends. More subtle forms are harder to fight because they're harder to see.

Social alienation is one of these indirect types. Social alienation isolates a person from his or her peers and makes the bullying target feel alone. Physical bullying is not usually involved, although verbal bullying might be included.

With social alienation, the bully's target is deliberately left out of activities. The bullies may stop speaking to the bullied person or stop responding when he or she speaks. When the target is around, the bullies may talk around him or her, making insulting or rude comments about the person as though he or she is not present. When the bullied person tries to defend himself or herself, the bullies may ignore the target. The bullies may also pressure the target's friends into going along with the bullying. Cell phones and text messaging can also be used to isolate and harass a bullied person.

Although bullies who take part in socially alienating behavior may not physically hurt the individual, their actions still cause harm. Any form of bullying damages the target's self-esteem. He or she may become lonely, anxious, and depressed.

The bullied person's behavior may change. He or she may stop eating or eat more than usual. Sleep patterns may also change, with the victim getting too much or too little sleep. The stress of being bullied can affect a person's health. Bullied people have been found to get sick frequently. They may go out of their way to avoid the bullies, even by cutting classes.

People who face social alienation often start withdrawing from others. They may stop taking part in activities that they once enjoyed because they feel shut out. For example, an actor in a school play may quit the production because he or she feels isolated by the obvious and deliberate refusal of others to acknowledge his or her successes or offer comfort for failures. The bullies accomplish their goal as the socially alienated person becomes withdrawn.

THE EFFECTS OF BEING BULLIED

Bullying can start at any point in school. Children may start bullying others as early as age four, usually in quarrels over toys or taking turns. As they age, bullies may start to focus on wanting to get their own way. They threaten others while playing so that they succeed in getting what they want. By the time children reach the third grade, they start to focus on the idea of treating others fairly. At this point,

Bullies often use gossip and rude comments to make their targets feel bad. The bullied person may not have the confidence to respond to such attacks.

bullies may start teasing other children, gossiping about them, or acting as though they are superior.

Some people become bullying targets very early in life. Once a pattern of bullying behavior is established, it can be hard to break. People can go through elementary school, middle school, and even high school as the victims of the same bullies.

Other people may become bullying targets later, when they reach middle school or high school. They may start out with a lot of friends, do well in their classes, play sports, and be popular with their peers. However, this can all change if a person is bullied.

In social alienation, targets are often popular students who are doing well, such as in coursework, music, or sports. The goal of the bully is to make the targeted person lose his or her sense of accomplishment and self-worth. The bully does this by isolating the target and pressuring others to do the same. The victim's accomplishments are diminished when he or she no longer gets respect and praise from others.

People who are bullied may constantly question their self-esteem. They lose confidence in their actions. They may feel that everything

PHOEBE PRINCE

Phoebe Prince was a fifteen-year-old who had emigrated with her family from Ireland to live in Massachusetts, where she attended South Hadley High School. After breaking up with her boyfriend, the boy and four other teens began a campaign of harassment against her that lasted for about three months. They threatened and insulted her, made slurs against her Irish ethnicity, and harassed her on Facebook. At times she was afraid of being attacked, and she often avoided class by going to the school nurse's office or skipping school.

Phoebe ultimately ended her own life by hanging herself at her home in January 2010. Authorities later said that on the day she committed suicide, one of her tormenters had written an extremely offensive word in place of Phoebe's name on a library sign-in sheet, and some of the teens had followed her home and mocked her while she cried.

The five teens involved in the bullying later pleaded guilty to misdemeanor charges and were sentenced to probation and community service. They had originally faced charges that could have brought jail time. Some criticized the sentence as being too light, while others felt that the teens should not have been charged at all.

they do is wrong and that they are being criticized all the time. As the person's sense of self-worth declines and he or she withdraws, friends may start pulling away and he or she loses their support.

Bullying is not limited to the school environment. Bullies can be found in programs, parks, neighborhoods, or any other social situation. Family members may bully other relatives. Even adults can be the victims of bullies at work.

HOW SOCIAL ALIENATION IS DAMAGING

All bullying is hurtful to the victim and to the bully. The pain caused by emotional bullying, such as social alienation, is also harmful—even if it does not leave physical marks. With social alienation and other forms of emotional bullying, it can be hard to show that the bullying is occurring.

People who experience social alienation see their former friends stop interacting with them and perhaps even join the bullies. They may hear their peers gossiping about them or spreading rumors. However, when they try to defend themselves, the bullies ignore their protests and continue their harassing behavior.

If a large group is taking part in the bullying, it may seem impossible to escape the bullies. In school, a person may have to endure several classes throughout the day with his or her tormentors. It may even be difficult to get away from the bullies in clubs, sports, and after-school activities, depending on how widespread the social alienation becomes. Things that the bullied person took pride in, such as grades, friends, or a particular skill or talent, may become focal points for bullies.

The bullied individual may try turning to a friend, only to find that the friend is no longer interested in talking to him or her. The friend may believe that by hanging out with the target, he or she may also become bullied. A bullied person might find that no one wants to sit with him or her at lunch or on the bus. Free time during the school

Former friends of a target can gang up on the target to exclude her or discourage her from taking part in school activities she once enjoyed. The targets of bullies may not know why the friendship ended.

day may be hard for the bullied person to take, as other kids either ignore or harass him or her. Even when alone, the bullies may reach out to harass their victim using cell phones, text messages, or social networks.

The bullied person may attempt to make new friends, only to discover that no one wants to be his or her friend. The individual may give up on forming new friendships that could break the cycle of bullying.

One bullied girl, who told her story on AboutHealth.com, described how her friends on the cheerleading team turned against her because she didn't behave like them. The other girls would be rude or hurtful toward her until she didn't want to go to school. The bullied girl reported that she was able to overcome the bullying once she realized that they only ganged up on her as a group and that by themselves they didn't have the courage to tell her what they believed. She also had a caring family who offered encouragement.

THE CONSEQUENCES OF BULLYING

Unfortunately, the bullying that a person experiences at school can follow him or her into adulthood. People who are shunned, left out of social activities, or the victims of rumors in school remember this treatment, and it can seep into later relationships. Psychologically, targets of social alienation often suffer from depression, anxiety, and feelings of loneliness in adulthood.

In a 2008 study, researchers from the University of Florida surveyed 210 college students between the ages of 18 and 25. They found that some people who had experienced social alienation were able to cope better if they had friends or other sources of positive support. Others seemed to have started believing what bullies said about them. These people were found to have more negative emotions that affected their ability to form positive relationships with others. Instead, they avoided meeting people and social situations that could have offered support.

MYTHS and FACTS

MYTH All bullying is physical.

FACT There are many forms of nonphysical bullying, including social alienation, verbal bullying, intimidation, and cyberbullying. A bully may use just one of these methods to intimidate his or her targets. A group of bullies may gang up to torment others in a variety of ways.

MYTH Bullies are always larger than their targets.

FACT Bullies often pick targets based on whether they are likely to resist, rather than on size alone. Bullies may come in all sizes and ages, and may even be the targets of other bullies.

MYTH Social alienation is less harmful than more direct forms of bullying.

FACT All bullying can cause lasting harm, even if the damage is not immediately obvious to others. Social alienation can crush a person's self-esteem and cause deep psychological scars.

CHAPTER 2

CREATING A BULLY

A bully is a person who harasses or acts aggressively toward another as a way of gaining power over that person or as a way to impress others. People may begin bullying at any age, though the pattern of bullying is often set when the person is very young. Some bullies grow out of their behavior. Others continue to make their classmates, coworkers, and neighbors miserable throughout their lives.

WHAT MAKES A BULLY?

Bullying can have numerous causes but often stems from self-esteem issues. The bully behaves aggressively as a way to deal with his or her own lack of self-respect. By dominating others and possibly gaining the admiration of peers, the bully may feel more self-confident.

Some bullies act aggressively because of problems at home. They may be abused or mistreated by a parent, an older sibling, or a caregiver. By gaining power over others, they may feel that

Physical bullying is the most visible way in which bullies intimidate their targets. Bullies often pick on others as a way to boost their own confidence.

they are making up for their lack of power at home. Or if they are not abused, they may be emotionally neglected. Their parents or care-givers may not pay enough attention to them. They may not actively abuse the bully, but emotional distance can also make a person feel unimportant.

Bullies can also be going through a rough time at home, even if they are treated well. Any number of events within a family can set off bullying behavior. Maybe the bully has a new sibling and is feel-ing left out. Or the bully's parents are divorcing. Money problems or other troubles could put stress on the family's life and cause a child to bully peers.

Some bullies may have been bullied themselves. For them, bullying is a way to regain their social standing. Bullies often feel that their own social standing is low and so they feel isolated. They want to win approval from their own friends and admiration from others. To do this, they pick targets that few of their peers would be willing to defend.

Bullies can be male or female. Male bullies tend to engage in more physical and direct forms of bullying. Female bullies are more likely to use indirect bullying tactics, such as social alienation. Male bullies do socially alienate their peers, although the physical forms of bullying usually come first.

GETTING AWAY WITH BULLYING

Successfully bullying someone may make a bully feel more confident. The bully may gain a sense of power over the target and a self-esteem boost from his or her friends. This is especially true of social alienation, where the bully can act like a leader by getting others to isolate a person.

Cell phones and social media can make it easier for bullies to isolate their targets without getting caught. Harassing e-mails and text messages can be sent using false names. Bullies may use their own names as a way to make their target feel more disconnected. A bully can also use the technology to organize others into bullying the target.

As the bully gets more confident, he or she may push the victim harder. With social alienation, this means that the bully may pressure more people into isolating the bullied person through taunts, rumors, and other tactics. For the bully, there can never be too much pressure applied to the target. As the pressure on the bullying target increases, so does the pressure on others to take part in the hostility.

The Internet and text messaging have all made it easier for bullies to taunt their targets without interference from teachers. Bullies can use smartphones to send harassing messages to others without giving their real names.

This is one reason why bullies are often able to get away with bullying behavior. People who want to defend the bullied individual may be discouraged from stopping or reporting the bullies. Instead, they become bystanders.

Bystanders may not like the bullying, but they do not act to stop it or attempt to befriend the bullied person. They may be afraid that they will also become objects of bullying if they try to stop it, or they may already be bullied themselves. They may see the socially alienated person as one of their few peers who is more unpopular than they themselves are.

Social pressure from peers also stops many bystanders from telling an adult that the bullying is taking place. They may be afraid that they will be the next target or they will be labeled as someone their peers can't trust and will be isolated, too.

The bullied person may also not want to tell an adult. That person may think that he or she will appear weak by telling adults about the bullying. People who are bullied may also be hesitant to tell someone about what is going on because they hope that the bullying will stop on its own. Or they may be afraid that it will get worse if they tell. With social alienation, bullies often choose people whom they envy to be their targets. The bully may hope to gain social status by finding a way to spoil the successes of his or her targets. The people bullies choose to target are often shy or lack confidence. They may not stand up for themselves or be able to find other ways to thwart the bully.

Even if the victims do tell, it can be hard to convince an adult that bullying is taking place. This is particularly true of social alienation because physical contact and verbal abuse aren't needed to isolate the victim. Teachers may not realize that a student is being socially alienated, or they may feel powerless to stop the behavior because no direct contact is taking place. Although they may be able to stop students from badgering or gossiping about their peers in class, they find it hard to stop someone from ignoring another person.

BEATING BULLYING HABITS

Bullies harass others as a way to improve their social standing and boost their self-esteem, but they may feel guilty or conflicted about their bullying. These feelings can lead to more bullying, rather than helping the bully end the behavior.

Bullying is not an unbreakable cycle, and bullies are capable of changing. A good way to start is for the bully to talk about the bullying behavior with a trusted adult, such as a parent or a guidance counselor, to figure out why he or she feels the need to bully. The bully may need to watch others to learn how to treat people with kindness and respect. Bullies with low self-esteem can boost their self-confidence through participation in a new activity or hobby. Making a close friend or two may also help a bully feel better without having to harass others.

WHAT HAPPENS TO BULLIES

Bullies don't necessarily remain bullies for their entire lives. Children who bully at a young age may grow out of the behavior as they mature. Those who start bullying as a way to deal with problems at home may stop once a situation has been resolved.

Some bullies never grow out of bullying. For these people, bullying may become so ingrained that they cannot stop. They learned that they could get what they wanted by bullying, so they never changed their behavior.

As these bullies grow older, some change their tactics. Bullies who were more physical may become more subtle. Instead of physically harassing their victims, they may engage in socially alienating tactics, such as spreading rumors or mocking the bullied person.

Long-term bullies may have other problems as well. Studies cited by the U.S. government show that bullies are more likely to abuse alcohol and other drugs and have criminal convictions and traffic citations as adults. They are also more likely to be abusive toward their spouses, children, or other loved ones when they are adults.

However, it is never too late to stop bullying. In May 2011, a Grand Rapids, Michigan, TV news program featured the story of sixty-five-year-old Andy Tomko. Tomko said that he had started bullying people when he was in the fifth grade and continued up into his twenties. One day he realized that he had acted as a bully and he decided to change his ways. He met with a therapist who encouraged him to share his story. He spent the next twelve years traveling the country, talking about his experiences, and telling students to treat others with kindness.

CHAPTER 3

BREAKING THE BULLYING CYCLE

Bullying is an imbalance of power between the bully and the bullied person. Sometimes the bully is the bigger or older of the two, but this is not always the case. Usually bullying victims have at least one characteristic that makes them stand out from or be rejected by the rest of their peers. This can be a physical characteristic, such as size, race, or the way the target talks, or it could be a personality trait. The bullied person could be extremely shy or socially awkward. A talent or particular skill that sets a person apart can lead to bullying, particularly if it is in an area that the bullies don't respect or in which the bully is jealous of the targeted victim's success.

HOW BULLIES CHOOSE TARGETS

People chosen as bullying targets may have easygoing personalities that cause them to tolerate extreme behavior in others, or

Targets often stop trying to defend themselves against people who engage in bullying. However, giving up may not stop social alienation and can even encourage bullies to push harder.

they may be unassertive and unwilling to defend themselves. They can be popular among some people and yet unpopular with others. Bullied people may not realize that they are disliked by a particular group until the bullying begins. With social alienation, the bullying can spread beyond just the bully's friends until the targeted person is ignored by many other peers, including people he or she considered friends.

DEVELOPING A DEFENSE

It may seem easy to give in to bullying or tempting to fight back physically. Fighting back, however, may get the target into trouble and give the bully the moral high ground to continue the alienating behavior. On the other hand, the targeted person might think that if he or she does what the bully wants, the bully will stop the attacks.

With social alienation, bullied people may drop activities they once enjoyed, stop hanging out with people they considered friends, and withdraw in the classroom. They may start missing school as a way to avoid the pain of social alienation, causing their grades to suffer. In extreme cases, the person who is bullied may transfer to another school or even drop out of school to avoid bullies.

It takes work to escape a bully. A bullied person has to try to put the bullying aside. People who become socially alienated by bullying may have personality traits that must be overcome so that they can beat bullying. They may be too passive, anxious, insecure, or sensitive. Bullying can bring these traits out and hide positive aspects of a person's personality.

Regaining confidence can be an important first step. Social alienation often damages a person's confidence, especially in the ability to make and keep friends. Bullied people have to make themselves visible in a positive way.

Bullied individuals who are already involved in school activities or sports should remain involved. Instead of focusing on the

Trying new activities can be a great way to make new friends. The targets of bullies can regain their confidence in the company of people who share their interests.

bullies, they might try to broaden their range of friends by hanging out with others who share their interests. The activity—whether it is music, sports, theater, clubs, or volunteer work—can help a bullied person take his or her mind off of the bullying. Getting to know people involved in the same activity and becoming friends with them can help boost a person's self-esteem. Deep bonds can form between sports teammates or cast members working together to stage a play.

WHO TO TELL

It is important for the target of bullying to tell someone he or she trusts and who can offer support. The bullied person should look to friends who can have a direct influence on peers. Have their friends defended them against bullies in the past, or have they acted as bystanders? Are the friends likely to mock the victim or tell others about the conversation? The bullied person should tell friends who can help him or her come up with a solution or who are willing to be supportive.

It may be harder to tell adults. Bullied people should let their parents know what is going on if they usually act encouraging. Teachers or coaches can also provide support and guidance. A therapist or guidance counselor may be able to help guide the victim as he or she works to regain self-esteem.

BUILDING RELATIONSHIPS

Building successful relationships can help restore a bullied person's confidence. More important, close friends can help fight off the social alienation tactics used by bullies. With luck, finding a few close friends will lead to more friends, as those first friends introduce the bully's target to their other friends.

However, not every attempt to reach out to make friends will work. The bullied person may reach out and be turned away several times. The pattern of rejection can be discouraging, and the bullied person may want to give up.

Developing relationships takes work and time. The people whom the target approaches may be shy. If they know about the social alienation, they may be wary of becoming friends out of fear that they, too, will become the objects of bullying.

If the bully's target is involved in a team sport or group activity, he or she may have an easier time making friends with other participants because they already share at least one interest. The target should take the time to figure out who might have the qualities he or she wants in a friend. Is the person generally friendly? Does the prospective friend have a good sense of humor or share the target's interests? The person who is bullied should find someone who matches up well with his or her personality.

The bullied person should also take things slowly once he or she has figured out who to befriend. Appearing overeager can drive the person away, but the target can't seem withdrawn or distant. If the person is someone he or she doesn't know well, the bullied person might begin with saying a simple "hello" and making small talk. There is nothing to lose by being friendly and polite. Even if the person does not want to become friends, he or she may remember the target as someone who is worthy of respect.

The bullied person should act confident when trying to make friends but avoid appearing overconfident. Others may be put off by someone who appears too cocky. It may be difficult to find the right balance between confidence and humility. If the target does something really well that earns praise from peers, such as playing a difficult solo, he or she should accept it gracefully, rather than brag about it. Be quick to praise others, but don't overdo it or it might seem as though the bullied person is trying to ingratiate himself or herself to others. If someone else helps the victim perform well, the target should be sure that he or she also gets credit. The other person will appreciate the acknowledgment of his or her role.

The bullied individual should try to stay positive and focus on social interactions that have gone well. He or she should be patient and keep trying. By making the effort, the bullied person can show that he or she is someone that others should want to get to know, rather than someone to ignore.

One way to show confidence is to be assertive in dealing with others. The bullied individual should suggest activities for his or her friends and take the first step in making connections. Don't wait for

Bullying targets can take steps to break away from their tormentors by reaching out to others. Sharing thoughts, jokes, and ideas with classmates can lead to friendships that are strong enough to endure social alienation.

them to call, but call them first with a suggestion, such as going to a game or to the movies. If they call first, be ready to go out and have a positive attitude about what the activity might be, even if it is something that you have never tried.

Humor can also be used to make friends and stump bullies. The bullying behavior may hurt deeply, but being able to laugh through the pain can confuse bullies. A sense of humor can also help a bullied person attract new friends. Others may come to admire a person who shows the inner strength to smile through a trying situation.

If it isn't possible to break the pattern of social alienation, it may be time to tell an adult. Parents or older relatives may not be able to help directly, but it can be comforting just to talk about one's problems.

Family members can help ease feelings of social alienation in more direct ways. Siblings or cousins close in age may be willing to hang out with the bullied person even when others aren't. They may introduce him or her to their own friends, opening up the possibility of forming friendships away from the bullies. Older relatives can also help. They may be able to introduce the bullied person to volunteer opportunities or group activities where the individual can meet other people and make new friends.

10 GREAT QUESTIONS
to ask a guidance counselor

1 How can I make new friends?

2 Should I tell my parents about feeling alienated?

3 Why won't my old friends hang out with me?

4 Does the school have an antibullying policy?

5 Where can I turn for help outside of school?

6 Will the bullies ever give up?

7 What can I do to make myself less of a target?

8 Should I talk to my teachers about how I feel isolated from other kids?

9 Is social alienation a big problem?

10 Will I still feel alienated after I leave school?

CHAPTER 4

OUT OF THE DARKNESS

For decades, bullying was considered a rite of passage that had to be endured. Children who were bullies were expected to grow out of bullying. Those who suffered the bullying were told to stand up for themselves and get through it because the experience would help build character.

Today, bullying is more widely seen as a common problem found in schools, workplaces, and other settings. People don't often recognize social alienating behavior as bullying unless they see it in the form of insults or gossip.

ALIENATION THROUGH BULLYING

Social alienation is a common result of many forms of indirect bullying. The damage caused by social alienation can be difficult to recognize. Bullying targets may avoid telling anyone about the situation. They may not ask for help in dealing with bullies

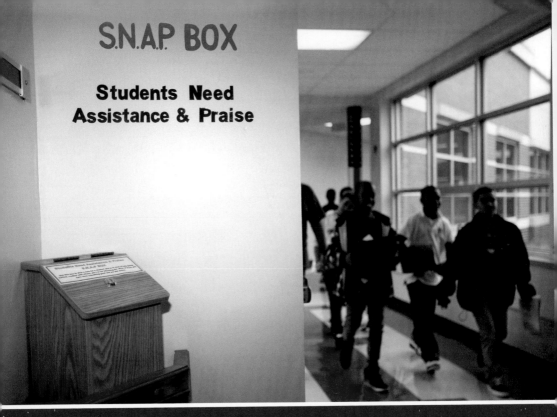

S.N.A.P. BOX

Students Need Assistance & Praise

Many schools have antibullying programs and a "bully box," which gives students a way to secretly report bullying incidents. Some programs focus on raising the self-esteem of students who are targets and teaching classmates and adults how to recognize bullying.

because they are afraid of appearing weak and unable to handle their own problems. Although friends or family members may see that there is a problem, they may not know what is causing the bullied person to withdraw.

Even if parents and friends know about the socially alienating behavior at school, they may not be able to stop it. Many schools have policies against bullying, but they may not be broad enough to cover social alienation. After all, it is hard to crack down on students who ignore their peers. Teachers and administrators may know about it but are unable to make it stop.

PROFESSOR DAN OLWEUS

Dan Olweus became a professor of psychology at the University of Bergen, Norway, in 1970. That year, he started what is known as the world's first scientific study of bully-and-victim conflicts among schoolchildren. In the 1980s, Olweus began focusing his research on bullying intervention.

Olweus's research led to the development of his Bullying Prevention Program and other initiatives aimed at ending bullying. In 1999, his program was chosen as a model for a national violence prevention initiative in the United States. His work has been widely recognized for bringing attention to bullying as a serious and harmful social problem.

There can be tremendous pressure not to report bullying. Bullies may threaten their targets and bystanders if their actions are reported. Many targets do not report bullying because they don't want to make the situation worse by angering the bully.

THE TRAGEDY OF SOCIAL ALIENATION

Some people may be able to ignore the bullying so successfully that the bullies give up. Other bullied individuals may take years to get over their mistreatment. Some never fully recover their confidence. Those who have been socially alienated may be extremely uneasy in social situations later in life, or they may completely avoid social activities.

A small number of people react to bullying by lashing out violently against their tormentors. They may fight with their bullies or become bullies themselves. In extreme cases, the target may feel so hopeless about his or her situation that he or she attempts suicide. "Bullycide" is the act of killing oneself as a result of bullying. Sadly, some of these attempts are successful. In the aftermath, people who knew the bullied person often reveal that they were aware of the bullying but could not stop it.

COMBATING BULLYING

A growing awareness of all forms of bullying has led schools and even state governments to take steps against bullying. Antibullying or antiharassment laws are in much of the United States. However, indirect bullying, like social alienation, is difficult to stop because it is mostly verbal and a lot of it can take place outside the classroom.

Many students are able to overcome bullying. Some go on to help others do the same. One such student is Blake Graham, who was bullied by his peers at his high school in Pawleys Island, South Carolina. Blake was isolated by people who mocked the way he dressed, talked, and acted. He learned to deal with the alienation, then decided that he wanted people to like him.

Blake changed the way he ate and began exercising. He lost weight and gained confidence. He began working hard to get good grades and dedicated himself to helping others in his community. He became involved in many activities and programs at his school. He wrote two antibullying books for teens to show the ill effects of bullying. As a teen ambassador for the national antibullying program Stomp Out Bullying, he works to educate others about the consequences of bullying.

During an appearance on a TV talk show in June 2011, singer and songwriter Taylor Swift spoke about being a victim of bullies when she was twelve and throughout her teens. She wrote the song "Mean," on her album *Speak Now* (2010), to bring awareness to the bullying issue and help others who had similar experiences to build self-confidence. She has said that she often felt isolated by peers when she was in school. What helped her get through it was that she knew she could write a song later to express her feelings.

Caitlin Uze has visited many schools to speak about how she was bullied as a seventh grader. As described in the *Martinsville*

Singer Taylor Swift has talked about being bullied when she was a teenager. Swift overcame these experiences and learned to pour out her emotions in songs.

Bulletin, Uze said that when she was young, she wore eyeglasses and braces, and she talked with a lisp. As Miss Virginia in 2010, Uze traveled around the state to speak frankly to middle and high school students about the dangers of bullying and how she worked with a speech therapist to improve her public speaking abilities. Although she still speaks with a bit of a lisp, she believes that it is not how you say something but what you have to say that counts. Both she and Swift offer stories of hope in beating bullying.

Dan Savage's It Gets Better Project has encouraged thousands of people to share their stories of overcoming bullying as a way to encourage bullied teenagers to look to the future.

Many organizations and programs work to curb or stop bullying. One of the most prominent programs is Dan Savage's It Gets Better Project. Savage and his husband, Terry Miller, launched the online video project in September 2010 in response to suicides by teens who were bullied because they were gay or because their peers suspected them of being gay. Since it was launched, more than twenty-two thousand videos from people of all sexual orientations have been uploaded to the site. Many celebrities have contributed to the project and its encouraging message that "it gets better."

A group of New Jersey middle school students created a video titled "Bullying: We'll Stop It." They made the video in response to news of the apparent suicide of Rutgers University freshman Tyler Clementi, who was a target of bullying.

The Council for Unity takes a more traditional approach to reducing bullying and violence in schools and communities. Since its founding in 1975, the group's hands-on methods have provided training to teach teens how to be responsible leaders in school and outside the classroom. The group also uses the arts—including painting and theater—to reenforce its curriculum. The group works to reach one hundred thousand young people from the ages of eight to twenty every year.

President Barack Obama's administration launched its own anti-bullying initiative. The Obama administration launched the Web site StopBullying.gov as a way to provide information on how young people, parents, teachers, and others can work together to stop bullying. Obama held summits to end bullying in 2010 and 2011, and made a video for the It Gets Better Project, along with other members of his administration. At the first conference, President Obama talked about being teased when he was young because of his ears and his unusual name. He told the audience that bullying can have destructive consequences for young people.

The work of these people and groups has raised awareness of all forms of bullying. More people now understand that social alienation is a serious problem. They also know that there are more places for people who are targets to go for help in beating bullies and making friends. With luck, even more people will be able to put their bullies behind them and look to a bright future.

abusive Extremely hurtful and insulting; engaging in violence and cruelty.

alienate To cause someone to feel isolated or cut off from others.

alienation The state of being an outsider or of feeling isolated, as from society.

anonymous Without any name acknowledged.

anxiety Distress or uneasiness of mind caused by fear of danger or misfortune.

belittle To make someone seem unimportant.

bully A person who hurts, persecutes, or intimidates others.

bystander A person present but not involved.

depression A mental condition marked by persistent gloom, feelings of inadequacy, and the inability to concentrate.

ethnicity The state of belonging to a social group that has a common national or cultural tradition.

ingratiate To bring oneself into favor with someone by flattering or trying to please the person.

initiative The act of taking charge before others do; the ability to start things independently.

misdemeanor A criminal offense, usually punishable by a fine, a jail term up to a year, or both.

passive Unresisting to external forces or influence.

peer A person who is equal to another in age, background, qualifications, abilities, and other categories.

probation A way of dealing with offenders by allowing them to go free under supervision of a probation officer.

subtle Not immediately obvious.

suicide The intentional taking of one's own life.

FOR MORE INFORMATION

BullyingCanada
471 Smythe Street
P.O. Box 27009
Fredericton, NB E3B 9M1
Canada
(877) 352-4497
Web site: http://www.bullyingcanada.ca
BullyingCanada is a Web site created by young people who speak
out about bullying and work to stop it.

Bullying.org
(403) 932-1748
Web site: http://www.bullying.org
This Canadian antibullying Web site was launched in 2000 in
response to a deadly school shooting in Taber, Alberta. It
provides information on bullying awareness.

National Bullying Prevention Center
PACER Center, Inc.
8161 Normandale Boulevard
Bloomington, MN 55437
(800) 537-2237
Web site: http://www.pacerteensagainstbullying.org
This center is committed to building awareness about bullying in
useful and creative ways.

National Crime Prevention Council
2001 Jefferson Davis Highway, Suite 901
Arlington, VA 22202-4801

(202) 466-6272

Web site: http://www.ncpc.org/topics/bullying

The National Crime Prevention Council provides resources on dealing with bullying.

Olweus Bullying Prevention Program

Institute on Family & Neighborhood Life

Clemson University

158 Poole Agricultural Center

Clemson, SC 29634

(864) 656-6712

Web site: http://www.clemson.edu/olweus

The Olweus Program's goals are to reduce and prevent bullying problems among schoolchildren and improve peer relations at schools.

Stop Bullying Now!

409 North Wayne Road

Wayne, ME 04284

Web site: http://www.stopbullyingnow.com

Stop Bullying Now! provides information on ending bullying in schools and communities. The Web site offers successul methods in bullying prevention.

U.S. Department of Health and Human Services

200 Independence Avenue SW

Washington, DC 20201

(877) 696-6775

Web site: http://www.hhs.gov

The U.S. Department of Health and Human Services works to protect the health and well-being of U.S. citizens. Its Office of Adolescent Health and teen Web site (http://stopbullying.gov) provide information about bullying, what to do to stop it, and where to go for help.

HOTLINES

Anti-Cyberbullying Hotline, Boston Public Health Commission (617) 534-5050
Boys Town National Hotline (800) 448-3000
CrisisLink (888) 644-5886
Kids Help Hotline (Canada) (800) 668-6868
KUTO Crisis Help (888) 644-5886 (KUTO stands for Kids Under Twenty One, but the hotline uses the abbreviation)
National Suicide Hotline (800) 784-2433
National Suicide Prevention Lifeline (800) 273-8255
National Youth Crisis Hotline (800) 448-4663
TEEN LINE (800) 852-8336
Trevor Lifeline for Gay, Lesbian, and Bisexual Youth (866) 488-7386
24-Hour Addiction Helpline (877) 579-0078
Youth America Hotline (877) 968-8454

WEB SITES

Due to the changing nature of Internet links, Rosen Publishing has developed an online list of Web sites related to the subject of this book. This site is updated regularly. Please use this link to access the list:

http://www.rosenlinks.com/beat/alien

FOR FURTHER READING

Burton, Bonnie. *Girls Against Girls: Why We Are Mean to Each Other and How We Can Change*. San Francisco, CA: Zest Books, 2009.

Gardner, Olivia, Emily Buder, and Sarah Buder. *Letters to a Bullied Girl: Messages of Healing and Hope*. New York, NY: HarperCollins, 2008.

Hall, Megan Kelley, and Carrie Jones. *Dear Bully: Seventy Authors Tell Their Stories*. New York, NY: HarperTeen, 2011.

Hutchings, Melinda. *It Will Get Better*. Crows Nest, NSW, Australia: Allen and Unwin, 2010.

Palmer, Pat, and Melissa Alberti Froehner. *Teen Esteem: A Self-Direction Manual for Young Adults*. Atascadero, CA: Impact Publishing, Inc., 2010.

Reid, Rhonda. *99 Things You Wish You Knew Before Facing a Bully*. New York, NY: The 99 Series, 2011.

Schab, Lisa. *Beyond the Blues: A Workbook to Help Teens Overcome Depression*. Oakland, CA: New Harbinger, 2008.

Shapiro, Ouisie. *Bullying and Me: Schoolyard Stories*. Chicago, IL: Albert Whitman & Company, 2010.

Simmons, Rachel. *Odd Girl Out*. Rev ed. Boston, MA: Mariner Books, 2011.

Sprague, Susan. *Coping with Cliques: A Workbook to Help Girls Deal with Gossip, Put-Downs, Bullying, and Other Mean Behavior*. Oakland, CA: New Harbinger, 2008.

Tarshis, Thomas Paul. *Living with Peer Pressure and Bullying*. New York, NY: Checkmark Books, 2010.

Withers, Jennie, and Phyliss Hendrickson. *Hey Back Off! Tips for Stopping Teen Harassment*. Far Hills, NJ: New Horizon Press, 2011.

BIBLIOGRAPHY

AboutHealth.com. "Bullying: Katti's Story." Retrieved November 30, 2011 (http://www.abouthealth.com/t_topicX.htm?topic=64).

Associated Press. "Obama: Bullying Shouldn't Be Part of Growing Up." March 10, 2011. Retrieved October 13, 2011 (http://www .msnbc.msn.com/id/42005402/ns/politics-white_house/t/ obama-bullying-shouldnt-be-inevitable-accepted).

Beane, Allan H. *Protect Your Child from Bullying*. San Francisco, CA: Jossey-Bass, 2008.

Birdwell, April Frawley. "Social Form of Bullying Linked to Depression, Anxiety in Adults." *University of Florida News*, April 22, 2008. Retrieved October 13, 2011 (http://news.ufl.edu/ 2008/04/22/bullying-2).

Carpenter, Deborah. *The Everything Parent's Guide to Dealing with Bullies*. Avon, MA: Adams Media, 2009.

Clark-Flory, Tracy. "Phoebe Prince's Bullies Get Bullied." Salon, April 8, 2010. Retrieved October 13, 2011 (http://www.salon .com/2010/04/08/phoebe_prince_bullies_get_bullied).

Clemson University. "Brief Information About Dan Olweus." August 8, 2011. Retrieved October 13, 2011 (http://www.clemson.edu/ olweus/history.htm).

Ellen DeGeneres Show. "Taylor Swift Shares Her Experiences Being Bullied." June 28, 2011. Retrieved November 30, 2011 (http://ellen.warnerbros.com/2011/06/taylor_swift_shares_her_ experiences_being_bullied_0628.php).

Garbarino, James, and Ellen deLara. *And Words Can Hurt Forever*. New York, NY: Free Press, 2003.

Hopson, Krista. "Why Do Some Kids Become Bullies?" University of Michigan Health System, January 7, 2002. Retrieved October 13,

2011 (http://www.med.umich.edu/opm/newspage/bullies.htm).

Khadaroo, Stacy Teicher. "Phoebe Prince Bullies Sentenced, But How Do They Make Things Right?" *Christian Science Monitor*, May 5, 2011. Retrieved October 13, 2011 (http://www .csmonitor.com/USA/Justice/2011/0505/Phoebe-Prince-bullies-sentenced-but-how-do-they-make-things-right).

Lines, Dennis. *The Bullies*. Philadelphia, PA: Jessica Kingsley Publishers, 2008.

Mann, Camille. "Mother of Phoebe Prince, Bullied Suicide Victim, Lashes Out in Mass. Court." *CBS News*, May 4, 2011. Retrieved October 13, 2011 (http://www.cbsnews.com/ 8301-504083_162-20059759-504083.html).

Melnick, Meredith. "Should We Rethink Our Anti-Bullying Strategy?" *Time*, September 28, 2011. Retrieved October 13, 2011 (http:// www.time.com/time/world/article/0,8599,2095423,00.html).

Nixon, Robin. "Studies Reveal Why Kids Get Bullied and Rejected." LiveScience.com, February 2, 2010. Retrieved October 13, 2011 (http://www.livescience.com/6032-studies-reveal-kids-bullied-rejected.html).

Pappas, Stephanie. "Behind Bullying: Why Kids Are So Cruel." LiveScience.com, April 9, 2010. Retrieved October 13, 2011 (http://www.livescience.com/6325-bullying-kids-cruel.html).

Pickhardt, Carl. *Why Good Kids Act Cruel*. Naperville, IL: Sourcebooks, 2010.

Sanders, Cheryl E., and Gary D. Phye, eds. *Bullying: Implications for the Classroom*. San Diego, CA: Elsevier Academic Press, 2004.

Sheras, Peter. *Your Child: Bully or Victim?* New York, NY: Skylight Press, 2002.

Tan, Sandra. "Teen Suicide Probe Looks at Charges in Bullying."
Buffalo News, September 22, 2011. Retrieved October 13, 2011
(http://www.buffalonews.com/city/communities/amherst/
article565876.ece).

Wayne, Suzanne. "Study Shows Bullying Affects Both Bystanders
and Target." HealthCanal.com, October 11, 2011. Retrieved
October 13, 2011 (http://www.healthcanal.com/mental-health-
behavior/21777-Study-shows-bullying-affects-both-bystanders-
and-target.html).

Winston, Eliza. "Miss Virginia Points to Her Past to Warn of
Bullying, Teasing." *Martinsville Bulletin*, March 20, 2011.
Retrieved November 30, 2011 (http://www.martinsvillebulletin
.com/article.cfm?ID=27778).

INDEX

ABOUT THE AUTHOR

As a volunteer elementary school tutor and peer counselor at his high school, Jason Porterfield witnessed many instances of social alienation and the pain caused by bullying. He is a journalist and writer living in Chicago, Illinois. He graduated from Oberlin College. He has written numerous books for young adults, including *Frequently Asked Questions About College and Career Training* and *Ritalin: A Difficult Choice.*

PHOTO CREDITS

Cover © istockphoto.com/Aldo Murillo; cover, interior graphics © istockphoto.com/aleksandar velasevic; p. 5 Mandy Godbehear/ Shutterstock.com; p. 7 Image Source/Getty Images; p. 9 BananaStock/Thinkstock; p. 12 Jupiterimages/Brand X Pictures/ Thinkstock; p. 16 © istockphoto.com/P_Wei; p. 18 © Maria Deseo/ PhotoEdit; p. 23 © istockphoto.com/1MoreCreative; p. 25 © istockphoto.com/AlbanyPictures; p. 28 © istockphoto.com/Steve Debenport; p. 32 © The Star-Ledger/Frances Micklow/The Image Works; p. 35 © Steve Marcus/Reuters /Landov; p. 36 Jason Szenes/ EPA /Landov; p. 37 © The Star-Ledger/Andy Mills/The Image Works.

Designer: Nicole Russo; Editor: Kathy Kuhtz Campbell;
Photo Researcher: Amy Feinberg